I0142433

A God Chat
The Art of Praying
Without Ceasing

Patricia Clarkson

A God Chat

The Art of Praying Without Ceasing

Copyright © 2025 by Patricia Clarkson

All rights reserved. No part of this book may be reproduced, distributed, or transmitted without written permission from the author or publisher, except for brief quotes in reviews or as permitted by copyright law.

This book reflects the author's personal opinions and interpretations and is for informational purposes only. It is not a substitute for professional advice. The author and publisher assume no liability for errors, omissions, or any consequences arising from its use. Any resemblance to actual persons, living or dead, is purely coincidental.

Scripture quotations taken from the (NASB®) New American Standard Bible®, Copyright © 1960, 1971, 1977, 1995, 2020 by The Lockman Foundation. Used by permission. All rights reserved. lockman.org

Printed in the United States of America

To my beloved husband, whose unwavering love, encouragement, and belief in me have been my steadfast foundation. You are my rock and my greatest blessing.

To my wonderful children, whose patience and support have inspired me to keep pursuing my dreams. Your love and laughter remind me daily of God's goodness.

And to the countless prayer warriors who have lifted me in prayer throughout this journey—your faith and intercession have been a source of strength and joy. This book is a testament to the power of God working through community and love. With deepest gratitude and love.

Table of Contents

Patricia Clarkson

PREFACE

Someone asked me to explain prayer. That request started an entire conversation about what prayer is and how to pray. It made me realize that if one person has questions, others would likely like to understand how to pray.

After much thought, prayers, and soul searching, I decided to write this book. I do not claim to be all-knowing or filled with endless wisdom. This book begins a journey to comprehend prayer and its significance in the life of every Christian.

Using the Lord's Prayer as a model, **Matthew 6:9-13 I** will delve into various styles of prayer, sharing some of my own experiences with each. I challenge you to dedicate time each day to practicing each prayer style presented in this book. Additionally, I encourage you to journal your thoughts on prayer using the provided pages. Each prayer is in the form of an everyday type of chat with a friend.

As you read and explore each style of prayer, you will begin to cultivate a deeper relationship with Christ. *May you continue to be blessed.*

INTRODUCTION

What is Prayer?

If you search online you will find the most common definitions of prayer as being communication with God, a request for help, praise, giving thanks, and the list of examples continues. For this book, I will define prayer as communication with God. We don't have to look up the definition of communicating. We know that one way of communicating is for one person to talk and another to listen. We know one person writes, the other reads, or we communicate through body language, then one person gestures and the other person reacts to the gestures. Once we understand the definition of communication, we realize that we are still communicating with God no matter how we pray.

Communication is important in our everyday life. We build relationships by communicating and interacting. We communicate with words and body language. Think about it: when you go to the store, you smile and say hello to different people. You are communicating. We build and maintain relationships by having an open line of communication. Therefore, to have a meaningful relationship with God, we must communicate with Him.

Communication is a two-way street. If you smile at someone and they frown or roll their eyes, they are communicating a different message than you are. Somehow, we understand the communication and act accordingly. We even communicate when we unfriend or ghost people. Hmmm... Sometimes we ghost God by not praying.

Preparing for Prayer

Throughout the Bible, there are examples of people communicating "praying" to God. In the New Testament Jesus provides us with a model prayer and some instructions. Most of us have memorized the prayer. But do we understand the model or template Jesus provided for us? Over the next few weeks, I will share seven types of prayers provided by Jesus in the Lord's Prayer.

Each example helps us become more aware when we pray. Regardless of which type of prayer you pray, there are some basics.

Matthew 6:5-8 provides the basics for how we enter into prayer.

And when you pray, you are not to be like the hypocrites; for they love to stand and pray in the synagogues and on the street corners so that they will be seen by people. Truly I say to you, they have their reward in full. But as for you, when you pray, go into your inner room, close your door, and pray to your Father who is in secret; and your Father who sees what is done in secret will reward you.

And when you are praying, do not use thoughtless repetition as the Gentiles do, for they think that they will be heard because of their many words. So do not be like them; for your Father knows what you need before you ask Him. Matthew 6:5-8

In plain words "Don't try to show off! We should not try to impress people with our powerful prayers. Remember, it is communication with God, not man.

For the most part, your personal communication with God (prayer) is a private act. I am not talking about when we pray at meetings or other gatherings. Those are public formal prayers. But even those do not require verbose prayers. We have all had the Thanksgiving or Christmas dinner where the person praying prays so long the poor turkey is cold. We are all saying Amen at various time intervals to try to help them conclude the prayer, but nooo, they just keep praying. Sometimes I think they must be hearing the song "Saints Don't Stop Praying For the Lord Is Nigh." When everyone else at the table is thinking Please Stop Praying the Turkey is dry.

It is important to remember who we are praying to and why we are praying then act accordingly. There is a time and place for public prayers and a time and place for private prayers. To everything, there is a season,

There is an appointed time for everything. And there is a time for every matter under heaven— A time to give birth and a time to die; A time to plant and a time to uproot what is planted. A time to kill and a time to heal; A time to tear down and a time to build up. A time to weep and a time to laugh; A time to mourn and a time to dance. A time to throw stones and a time to gather stones; A time to embrace and a time to shun embracing. A time to search and a time to give up as lost; A time to keep and a time to throw away. A time to tear apart and a time to sew together;

A time to be silent and a time to speak. A time to love and a time to hate; A time for war and a time for peace. Ecclesiastes 3:1-8.

How often do we pray?

How often we pray is really up to the individual. Yes, the scripture says to *pray without ceasing 1 Thessalonians 5:17,* but what does that mean? Do we walk around all day, every day, just spouting out prayers? I know a person who loudly prays while shopping. You can hear them aisles away. Another friend lays their hands on every item at the store that they are considering buying. They pray for guidance on whether to buy the item or not. That could easily turn into a very long shopping trip. Is that what 1 Thessalonians 5:17 means? Some scholars would argue, yes, that is exactly what it means others have another interpretation. How can we pray without ceasing in the proverbial closet mentioned in Matthew 6.6? For me, the closet is a corner of my mind. Have you noticed you can be talking with someone and be thinking of something else at the same time? Perhaps you are cleaning the house, mowing the lawn, or another routine activity and you are also thinking about something else. Our minds are powerful and can do two things at once. I used to tell my students there is a cool thing that our brains can do. It can see words and understand them without using your mouth. Well, today I want to share another cool thing our brain can do. Our brain can allow our body to work and still think about something else. I call this "moving meditation" or "functioning prayer." So yes, we should pray without ceasing.

Dedicate a corner of your mind to functioning prayer. You will also need a physical private place to pray. My proverbial closet is a rocking chair. I sit and have a real conversation with God. I sit and pray, talk, listen, cry, laugh, and do whatever I need to do when communicating with God. My second closet is my garden, and my third closet is anywhere I can find private and quiet. As you can see you can have several closets.

I do not know about you but, I am a squirrel chaser (I get distracted). I need quiet time to talk with God. I get up at 5:30 a.m. almost every morning to have that quiet time with God. The house is quiet. The world is quiet. After my quiet time with God, I have a cup of coffee and watch the sunrise. The wonder of the breaking of the day never ceases to take my breath away.

I am the type of person that will keep going 7 days a week. I must remember to slow down and rest. By resting I regenerated my mind and body. I once hired a trainer to help me build muscle and maintain bone density. He shared the importance of not lifting weights using the same muscles every day. The body needs recovery time. Without recovery time, I am doing more damage than good to my muscles.

I see this concept in the Bible.

By the seventh day God completed His work which He had done, and He rested on the seventh day from all His work which He had done. 3 Then God blessed the seventh day and sanctified it, because on it He rested from all His work which God had created and made. Genesis 2:2-3

Now, let's wash our face, find our secret closet, and get down to the business of praying. Having a high-quality conversation with God. My prayer journal journey begins here.

Each day, I will rise early, wash my face, and pray throughout the day using the template of the week for six days, and on the seventh day, I will rest (Be still and know that He is God).

A God Chat

WEEK 1

The Art of Reverence

Beginning a Conversation with God

Our Father who is in heaven, Hallowed be your name. Matthew 6:9

Greetings, Praise, and Acknowledgement

The Lord's Prayer has been studied and memorized countless times. During the first week of my prayer reset journey, I began using this scripture alone as a form of prayer. I needed God in different ways during various times in my life. I am grateful He was always there meeting my needs. As I reflected on the various attributes of God my soul rejoiced.

I am terrible at remembering people's names. I will remember details about conversations and other information about them, but names seem to escape my mind. A good friend told me people feel more connected to you when you speak their name. They know that you recognize them. I try very hard to say a person's name several times to remember it. I consider this a sign of respect. By saying a person's name, I am acknowledging them.

As a child, I learned to greet people when I entered a room. This verse reminds me that even when praying I need to greet God first, by his name. If I start talking in a room with several people, how do they know who am I talking to? Do I look at them? Do I call them by name? Do I stand close enough so there can be no doubt that I am talking to them? The best way to let them know I am talking to them is to call them by their name.

This is exactly what the first section of **Matthew 6:9** is modeling. ***Our Father who is in Heaven.*** As I begin each prayer, I will begin by honoring the divine entity I am speaking with, exclusively, by name. I know this sounds strange. Of course, I know I am talking to God.

But does every other spiritual entity in the atmosphere know that? Maybe some spiritual entities are like some people who jump into your conversations or business, and you must remind them that you are not talking to them.

For our struggle is not against flesh and blood, but against the rulers, against the powers, against the world forces of this darkness, against the spiritual forces of wickedness in the heavenly places. Ephesians 6:12

We cannot forget Satan is a spirit and there are other fallen angels. They can see and hear us. We need to be clear about who we are speaking with.

Be of sober spirit, be on the alert. Your adversary, the devil, prowls around like a roaring lion, seeking someone to devour. 1 Peter 5:8

Here is the next part of this prayer, *"Hallowed be Your name."*

Cambridge Dictionary defines Hallowed

1. Very respected and praised because of great importance or great age:

2. holy

3. Highly respected.

I also referenced other Biblical translations to understand the phrase better.

- ... Your name be honored as holy. (CSB)
- ... Uphold the holiness of your name. (CEB)
- ... May your Name be kept holy. (CJB)
- ... Help us to honor your name. (CEV)
- .... let thy name be sanctified, (DARBY)

There is an old song I used to hear almost every Sunday at church. It is a Congregational Praise Song:

> *Bless that wonderful name of Jesus*
> *Bless that wonderful name of Jesus*
> *Bless that wonderful name of Jesus*

*No other na*me **I know**

This may not technically be a prayer, but it is a powerful opening to every prayer. Mastering the art of blessing and reverence is important to everyone's prayer life.

During the first week of prayer, I will spend time honoring and reverencing God. What is the difference between honoring and reverencing God?

Honor may apply to the recognition of one's right to great respect … reverence implies profound respect mingled with love, devotion and awe. *www.merriam-webster.com/dictionary*

There are so many attributes of God. He is called by different attributes based on the needs of the people and the actions of God. Table 1 lists some of the attributes of God. Each day I will select two of the attributes to focus on. As you embark on this prayer journey, I encourage you to select the attributes that resonate with you daily. As you go through the day look for these attributes in the world around you and in your own life. Each time you see or feel the attribute take a few seconds to acknowledge it and revere the Lord.

...For yours is the kingdom and the power and the glory forever Matthew 6:13c

By acknowledging God's greatness and power we humble ourselves before Him. He has the final say in what is and what is not to be.

There is an activity called "Trust Falls" where someone or a group stands behind you and you free fall backward trusting that they will catch you. Well, I never trusted they would catch me. I refused to participate in that activity. Yet when it comes to trusting God that is exactly what we must do. Trust that he is always there to catch us. It is by his power, by his might that we move forward and successfully through life.

... Not by might nor by power, but by My Spirit,' says the Lord of armies. Zachariah 4:6

As we journey through life we work, play, make plans, and do the best we can to move forward each day. We know *faith without works is dead James 2:26.* So we work exercising our faith that our efforts will bear fruit.

Commit your works to the Lord, And your plans will be established Proverbs 16:3

When we work and yield, yield and work, we allow God to water and fertilize our labor.

Oftentimes we yield but do not work. We want God to give while we do nothing but take. That is not how it works.

This week explores the art of opening and closing prayers effectively. Mastering the art of prayer opening and closing is true food for the soul. Practice makes perfect. I think about sports. Athletes practice drills over and over until the movements are muscle memory. Today people are encouraged to recite mantras. Why are mantras so popular? Because if you say something over and over again it becomes a part of who you are and how you think. We all know that how you think is how you will act.

By mastering the art of praising, honoring, reverencing, and acknowledging God we feed our soul and mind. It will become a part of who we are.

I cannot think of a better way to begin reframing my thoughts and actions than by opening a conversation with God and acknowledging that he has all power.

Each time I sing this song I think of the character traits or attributes of God. I get excited about who He is and I cannot help but worship Him. I know the full lyrics of this song only mention Nissi, Shalom, and Jireh, but as I honored God this week, I sang this song each day with the attributes I chose for the day.

... Because of who you are, I give you glory

Because of who you are, I give you praise

Because of who you are, I will lift my voice and

say

Lord, I worship you because of who you are

Songwriters: Brian Kelly McKnight / Michael Brandon Barnes

Table 1

NAME / ATTRIBUTE	MEANING
Abba	Father
Adonai	Lord, Master
Alpha and Omega	The Beginning and End
El Chay	The Living God
El Chuwl	The God Who Gave You Birth
El Deah	The God of Knowledge
El Elyon	The Most High God
El Gibhor	The Mighty God
El Olam	The Everlasting God
El Roi	The God Who Sees
El Shaddai	Lord God Almighty
Elohim	God
Immanuel	God With Us
Yahweh / Jehovah	God

Table 1

NAME / ATTRIBUTE	MEANING
Yahweh / Jehovah	God
Jehovah Jireh	The Lord Will Provide
Jehovah Mekoddishkem / M'Kaddesh / Mekadesh	The Lord Who Sanctifies
Jehovah Nissi	The Lord My Banner
Jehovah Rapha	The Lord That Heals
Jehovah Sabaoth	The Lord of Hosts
Jehovah Shalom	The Lord Is Peace
Jehovah Shammah	The Lord Is There
Jehovah Tsidkenu	The Lord Our Righteousness
Jehovah Tsuri	The Lord Our Rock
Jehovah-Bore	The Lord Creator
Jehovah-Raah / Rohi	The Lord My / Our Shepherd

Reflection

WEEK 1 / Day 1

The Art of Reverence

Beginning a Conversation with God

Our Father, who is in heaven, Hallowed be Your name. Matthew 6:9

What two or three names or attributes will you focus on today?

How might your understanding of the attributes of God influence your daily interactions and prayers?

Reflection

WEEK 1 / Day 2

The Art of Reverence

Beginning a Conversation with God

Our Father, who is in heaven, Hallowed be Your name. Matthew 6:9

What two or three names or attributes will you focus on today?

What did you notice throughout the day as you praised and honored God focusing on His attributes?

Reflection

WEEK 1 / Day 3

The Art of Reverence

Beginning a Conversation with God

Our Father, who is in heaven, Hallowed be Your name. Matthew 6:9

What two or three names or attributes will you focus on today?

What other steps can you take to ensure clarity and reverence when communicating with God

Reflection

WEEK 1 / Day 4

The Art of Reverence

Beginning a Conversation with God

Our Father, who is in heaven, Hallowed be Your name. Matthew 6:9

What two or three names or attributes will you focus on today?

What are some things you noticed throughout the day as you praised and honored God?

Reflection

WEEK 1 / Day 5

The Art of Reverence

Beginning a Conversation with God

Our Father, who is in heaven, Hallowed be Your name. Matthew 6:9

What two or three names or attributes will you focus on today?

What specific practices or rituals could you adopt as part of your daily routine to ensure you acknowledge the various aspects of God?

Reflection

WEEK 1 / Day 6

The Art of Reverence

Beginning a Conversation with God

Our Father, who is in heaven, Hallowed be Your name. Matthew 6:9

What two or three names or attributes will you focus on today?

How do you feel your relationship with God has evolved as you've focused on referencing Him?

REFLECTION

WEEK 1 / Day 7

The Art of Reverence

Beginning a Conversation with God

Our Father, who is in heaven, Hallowed be Your name. Matthew 6:9

Rest / Reflect / Meditate / Listen

Congratulations you have honored and praised the name of God for six days. During that time, you have deepened your understanding of what each attribute means in your life. You have seen his power and wonder each day.

God created the earth in six days. On the seventh day, he rested.

By the seventh day, God completed His work which He had done, and He rested on the seventh day from all His work which He had done. 3 Then God blessed the seventh day and sanctified it because on it He rested from all His work which God had created [a]and made. Genesis 2:2-3

Take this seventh day to rest and reflect on what you experienced by just reverencing, honoring, and praising God all week. You did not ask for things during those moments. You simply enjoyed the glory of God. This is a great time to be still and hear the voice of God in your heart. Feel his presence around you.

Stop striving (let go, relax) and know that I am God; I will be exalted among the nations, I will be exalted on the earth. Psalm 46:10

How does the act of worshiping God for His attributes impact your spiritual mindset and daily actions?

A God Chat

WEEK 2

Seeking God's Kingdom

Embracing Purpose and Spiritual Growth

Your kingdom come. Your will be done, on earth as it is in heaven. Matthew 6:10

Yielding Your Will

Week 2 Part 1

Your kingdom come, ... Matthew 6:10a

What a powerful prayer! Often, when we recite the Lord's Prayer, we rush through this verse without pausing to contemplate its meaning or at least its significance to us. There are two ways to view Matthew 6:10. This verse could be interpreted referring to the Second Coming. If that is the case, we are asking God to establish His kingdom on earth and are eagerly awaiting His arrival. We can also interpret this scripture as we are the body of Christ; thus, the kingdom is in us. If that is the case, then we are asking God to shape us into the image of the Kingdom. Throughout the Bible, there are references to the kingdom of God.

But seek first His kingdom and His righteousness,…
Matthew 6:33

But seek His kingdom, and these things will be provided to you. 32 Do not be afraid, little flock, because your Father has chosen to give you the kingdom. Luke 12:31-32

Now you are Christ's body, and individually parts of it.… 1 Corinthians 12:27

Now He was questioned by the Pharisees as to when the kingdom of God was coming, and He answered them and said, "The kingdom of God is not coming with signs that can be observed; 21 nor will they say, 'Look, here it is!' or, 'There it is!' For behold, the kingdom of God is in your midst." Luke 17:20-21

The Kingdom of God is within each of us. As we pray, we are asking God to shape us into a reflection of His kingdom. We are the body of Christ and a reflection of the Kingdom of God. The Kingdom of God is in us! When we pray this week, we are asking that our life reflect the Kingdom of God right here right now on earth. We are asking God to come into our lives and allow His kingdom to dwell in us.

It may be difficult at times for all the Kingdom of God to flow through you. God understands the struggle humans have with fleshly desires. That is why God sent the Comforter to help us understand how to be a living example of the Kingdom of God. We still have a choice. We can allow the Comforter to lead and guide us or discard the guidance. The choice is ours.

But the Helper, the Holy Spirit whom the Father will send in My name, He will teach you all things, and remind you of all that I said to you. John 14:26

As a child and during my young adult years, my parents, teachers, and other adults provided me with guidance. They shared their wisdom and knowledge with me in hopes that I would take it and be successful. I remember, at times, I thought their advice was old and outdated. I felt that they did not know what they were talking about. I thought the era of time I was in was different from when they were growing up. They didn't even have the internet. They had black and white TV. Their phones were attached to the wall. They were old and outdated people with outdated wisdom and knowledge. How could they possibly understand what I was going through?

What has been, it is what will be, And what has been done, it is what will be done. So there is nothing new under the sun. Ecclesiastes 1:9

Technology has changed and society moves quickly, but human behavior and desires are the same. The wisdom of the ages is steadfast.

This week let us look inward and begin building our inner Kingdom of God. Let us take the advice of the Comforter. God knows our flaws and is loving enough to help us grow. Well...that is if we are willing to listen.

When my husband and I bought our first home we were so excited. It was not in the best neighborhood nor was the house in the best shape. But it was what we could afford, and it was ours. We didn't have money to pay a carpenter, electrician, or plumber. There was no Google or YouTube to help us learn to repair the house. There were books with words and pictures. There was a local hardware store with knowledgeable employees. We took inventory of what needed repairs. We prioritized the repairs based on needs and money. We learned basic plumbing. We learned how to change plugs and light fixtures. We learned how to drywall. We learned about load-bearing walls. By the time we sold the house, we had completed extensive renovations with the help of a few good friends. We were open to listening, learning, and making mistakes. When we open our hearts and minds to the leading of the Comforter can successfully make extensive renovations in our spiritual lives.

As we begin this part of the prayer, we will need to take inventory of who we are and where we are in our lives. Listen to the voice of God and begin the process of renovating our lives. We are all unique. We will need different spiritual adjustments. Maybe we need to view situations with open minds and hearts. We may need to re-evaluate who we choose to surround ourselves with. You and God are the only ones who truly know what you need to be a shining example of the Kingdom of God. People will try to tell you what you need. Some will prophesy to you. But this week's prayer is about you and God and only you and God. Allow Him to build His Kingdom in your life. Allow him to restore His temple, yes that temple is you!

Do you not know that you are a temple of
God and that the Spirit of God dwells in
you? 1 Corinthians 3:16

It is so exciting when someone "lays hands" on us and prophecies wonderful things. It is so awesome when the preacher tells us exactly what we want to hear.

This week is not about that "super fantastic thing"that"wow moment." It is not about tears, rolling on the floor, snot, dancing, prancing, or any amazing fanfare. This is a conversation between you and your creator. It is about allowing Him to remodel you. You want to hear from Him.

Table 2 lists examples of the Kingdom of God. Taking time to read several examples of the Kingdom of God will help you understand what you are asking when you pray, "Thy Kingdom come."

Kingdom of God / Heaven Parables	
Parable	**Scriptures**
Sower	Matthew 13:3-23
Weeds	Matthew 13:24-30
Mustard Seed	Matthew 13: 31-32
Yeast	Matthew 13:33
Hidden Treasure	Matthew 13:44
Pearl	Matthew 13:45-46
Net	Matthew 13:47-50
Householder	Matthew 13:52
Unforgiving Servant	Matthew 18:23-31
Vineyard Workers	Matthew 20:1-16
Two Sons	Matthew 21:28-32
Wedding Banquet	Matthew 22:1-14
Ten Virgins	Matthew 25-1-13
Planting	Mark 4:26-29
Within You	Luke17:20-21

Week 2 - Part 2

let's take a look at the second part of the verse.

Your will be done, on earth as it is in heaven.

— Matthew 6:10b

God created the heavens and the earth in six days. He put certain things into motion. If you watch any of the Animal Kingdom shows, you will notice that the animals follow certain behavioral patterns. Plants follow a certain order. Insects stay true to who and what they are. God created them a certain way, and they follow His will. They have no choice but to follow the will or plan God put in place for them.

Praise Him, sun and moon; Praise Him, all stars of light!
Praise Him, highest heavens, And the waters that are above the heavens!
They are to praise the name of the Lord, For He commanded, and they were created. He has also established them forever and ever; He has made a decree, and it will not pass away. Praise the Lord from the earth, Sea monsters, and all the ocean depths; Fire and hail, snow and clouds; Stormy wind, fulfilling His word; Mountains and all hills; Fruit

trees and all cedars; Animals and all cattle; Crawling things and winged fowl; — Psalm 148:3-10

God put a plan in place for each of us. The difference between the rest of creation and us is that we have a choice. We can follow the plan or choose another path.

We talk about the will of God. We say, "Have your way, Lord." But do we know what His will is for our individual lives? What does God want you to do? Not everyone is a preacher, teacher, or missionary. Not everyone is going to be in the spotlight.

"Before I formed you in the womb I knew you, And before you were born I consecrated you; I have appointed you as a prophet to the nations." — Jeremiah 1:5 "For I know the plans that I have for you," declares the Lord, "plans for prosperity and not for disaster, to give you a future and a hope." — Jeremiah 29:11

God knew Jeremiah before he was born. God knew what He wanted Jeremiah to do. He had a specific purpose for Jeremiah's existence. Oh, I am quite sure when Jeremiah was a child, he ran and played like most children do. He laughed and gave no real thought to his purpose in life. But as he grew and matured, his focus changed, and he stepped into his calling—his purpose, his reason for being. Some theologians say Jeremiah was about 20 when he stepped into his purpose. I do not know how accurate that information is. What I do know is that Jeremiah was not comfortable speaking. But God encouraged him.

Then I said, "Oh, Lord God! Behold, I do not know how to speak, Because I am a youth." But the Lord said to me, "Do not say, 'I am a youth,' Because everywhere I send you, you shall go, And all that I command you, you shall speak." — Jeremiah 1:6-7

God knew us before we were born. We were not born by accident. We each have a purpose. Do you know the plans God has for you? What is your purpose for being on earth at this time in history? What impact will you make on the world? We do not all need to have a statue built in our honor. We do not all need to be in the front with accolades. We may just be the one domino that causes a wonderful chain reaction. We do not always know the lives we touch, for good or for bad.

Can you walk in the purpose God has given you and be content with your journey? Are you truly willing to allow His will to be done in your life as it is in heaven?

As you pray this week, the focus is on the inner you. This is not about big life changes. It is about taking inventory and making adjustments or refinements to the inner you. You may be at ground zero, or you may just need a fresh coat of paint. Only you and God know. I challenge you to enter this week with an open heart and mind. Chat with God, and pause to listen for answers and signs. Yield to His will.

Prayer Instructions

Day 1-2 – Your Kingdom Come

The first two days, you are only praying, "Thy Kingdom Come." Your prayer will focus on understanding the Kingdom of Heaven and how it relates to you. What is the Kingdom of Heaven like? When you pray, "Thy Kingdom Come," begin to reflect on what you are asking to happen. Chat with God about what you are truly asking when you pray, "Thy Kingdom Come." Feel the request deep in the core of your being. Take time during the week to read some of the kingdom parables.

Day 3-4 – Your Will Be Done

Yield yourself to be made into the image of His Kingdom. Do not try to second-guess what God wants to do in your life. Allow the Master Builder to begin the remodeling process in your heart, mind, and soul. You might not know what is happening, or you might not feel anything. Just trust that if you yield, the change will occur. Sometimes God will take a sledgehammer and knock down the walls. Sometimes He will use sandpaper to smooth out rough edges. Other times, it may be a gentle dusting off of a little dirt. Allow God to do His thing. Do not jump in and try to help Him out. Just yield.

Day 5-6 – On Earth As It Is In Heaven (In Me As It Is In   Heaven)

During this section of the prayer, focus on allowing God to guide you to your purpose. Allow the Comforter to teach you God's will in your life. Begin the slow or fast release of your will to fully yield to God's will. This is an important and powerful prayer. Asking for His perfect will in your life can be scary. What if it is not what you expect? What if it is hard? But think about the reward and the end product of your life. Whatever His will is for you, it is amazing! Before you pray, read *Jeremiah 29:11* and *Psalm 32:8*. May you be blessed.

Reflection

Seeking God's Kingdom
Embracing Purpose and Spiritual Growth
Your kingdom come. Your will be done on earth, as it is in heaven. – Matthew 6:10

Your Kingdom Come - As you pray (**God Chat**), allow the Comforter to help you understand the depth of the parables.

As you prepare for the focused prayer on "Thy Will Be Done," what intentions or expectations do you have? How will you stay open to the guidance you receive?

Reflection

WEEK 2 - DAY 2

Seeking God's Kingdom

Embracing Purpose and Spiritual Growth

Your kingdom come. Your will be done on earth, as it is in heaven. – Matthew 6:10

Your Kingdom Come - What adjustments might you need to make to align more closely with God's Kingdom?

How do you personally interpret "Thy kingdom come" in your prayer life? Do you lean more toward a literal expectation of the Second Coming or a personal, internal transformation?

Reflect on Matthew 6:33 and Luke 17:20-21. How do these verses shape your understanding of what it means to seek and embody the Kingdom of God?

Reflection

WEEK 2 - DAY 3

Seeking God's Kingdom

Embracing Purpose and Spiritual Growth

Your kingdom come. Your will be done on earth, as it is in heaven. – Matthew 6:10

Your Will Be Done- Allow the Comforter (the Spirit of God) to minister to your soul. Are there areas where you feel uncertain about God's will? This is the time to chat with God about His will in your life. Remember, His will may or may not include being a superstar. How will you approach seeking clarity?

What mindset or attitude adjustments might help you yield more fully to God's will during this time of introspection?

Reflection

Seeking God's Kingdom

Embracing Purpose and Spiritual Growth

Your kingdom come. Your will be done on earth, as it is in heaven. – Matthew 6:10

Your Will Be Done- How do you approach the uncertainty of not knowing exactly what God's will for you might be?

How can you cultivate a sense of peace and excitement about this uncertainty?

Reflection

Week 2 Day 5

Seeking God's Kingdom

Embracing Purpose and Spiritual Growth

Your kingdom come. Your will be done on earth, as it is in heaven. – Matthew 6:10

On Earth As It Is In Heaven- Take 5-10 minutes to observe the plants, vegetation, insects, and animals around you. How are they fulfilling the will of God? Every living thing yields to the will of God. They fulfill the purpose God created them for. *(Genesis 1:11-12)*

How does the concept of God knowing you before you were born influence your understanding of your purpose?

How do the people you surround yourself with impact your spiritual journey? Are there relationships you need to reevaluate in light of seeking the Kingdom of God?

Reflection

WEEK 2 - DAY 6

Seeking God's Kingdom
Embracing Purpose and Spiritual Growth
Your kingdom come. Your will be done on earth, as it is in heaven. – Matthew 6:10

On Earth As It Is In Heaven - How can you deepen your trust in God's plan for your life, even when it may not align with societal expectations or personal ambitions?

How has actively listening to God and seeking His guidance affected your spiritual growth and daily life? Can you identify specific ways in which your life has been transformed?

Reflection

WEEK 2 DAY 7

Seeking God's Kingdom
Embracing Purpose and Spiritual Growth
Your kingdom come. Your will be done on earth, as it is in heaven. – Matthew 6:10

Congratulations! You have focused solely on the will of God this week. You have taken time to notice God's wonderful creations and how they yield to His will. You have taken steps to yield your life to His will.

Take this seventh day to rest and reflect on what you have experienced.

How do the promises in *Jeremiah 29:11* and *Psalm 32:8* encourage and reassure you about God's plans for your life? How can these promises support you in your journey?

How will you continue to cultivate a personal, ongoing conversation with God about His will in your life?

How do you listen for and discern God's guidance in your life? Are there specific practices or methods that have helped you in the past?

WEEK 3

Daily Bread and Beyond

Balancing Necessities and Desires

"Give us this day our daily bread." — Matthew 6:11

Many of our prayers are consumed with our needs. "Lord, I need this. Lord, I need that." We need so many things in life—a place to live, transportation, food, clothes—the list goes on. Sometimes, we believe we need a new phone, car, or house to appear successful. However, it is important to distinguish between our basic needs and our wants.

Before computers, television, and radio, our wants were limited to what we saw around us, read in newspaper ads, or were convinced we needed by door-to-door salespeople. Technology now provides us with endless opportunities to see and want more. Advertisements create a constant sense of longing.

At times, it may be challenging to differentiate between needs and wants. So, what exactly is our "daily bread"? Bread has been a staple food in every society for at least 30,000 years and symbolizes our basic needs.

It is interesting to hear people define what constitutes basic needs. Depending on one's social status, this definition may vary. For consistency, we will use Maslow's Hierarchy of Needs as a guide to understanding different levels of necessity.

Maslow's Hierarchy of Needs categorizes human necessities into five levels. The theory argues that the two most fundamental levels must be met before an individual can progress to psychological needs. To reach self-actualization or fulfillment, all four preceding levels must be satisfied to some degree. (1) This week, we will take a personal inventory to determine where we should begin our prayers.

Let's take some time to reflect on our basic needs. Once we have our "Daily Bread," we are ready to evaluate our desires beyond basic needs. Here is a simple checklist to see which basic needs you already have.

Maslow's Hierarchy of Needs

SELF-ACTUALIZATION
Be all you can be

SELF ESTEEM
Dignity, Achievement, Mastery, Independence, Respect, Status

LOVE / BELONGING
Family, Friendship, Intimacy, Trust, Acceptance

SAFETY
Protection from elements, Security, Employment, Financial Stability

Physiological
Air, Food, Water, Shelter, Clothes

Physiological Checklist:

- Water

- Shelter (house, apartment, protection from the elements, etc.)

- Healthy Food (It may not be your favorite, but it should be healthy and edible)

- Clothes for the proper season (Secondhand clothes are fine)

- Shoes for the proper season (Gently reused are fine)

Safety Checklist:

- Protection from the elements
- Employment or a means of income
- Personal security
- Health

Basic needs sustain life. **Matthew 6:11** clearly states: "Our daily bread," not our daily prime rib steak, a private jet, or any other luxury item we can think of. Basic needs do not have to be fancy. Shelter does not have to be a three-story house on two acres of land. It does not have to be a condominium with a view of a lake or ocean.

How our physiological and safety needs are met is determined by our phase of life. As children, our parents or guardians provide most of these needs. As we became adults, we found that we were expected to be self-sufficient. We work and pursue avenues to secure our daily bread. We trust God to be with us every step of the way. We know God's eye is on the sparrow as well as us. He will provide.

As you pray for the two basic levels of needs, know that God will answer your prayers.

But if God so clothes the grass of the field, which is alive today and tomorrow is thrown into the furnace, will He not much more clothe you? You of little faith! (Matthew 6:30)

When the Israelites were in the wilderness, God provided their daily bread and protein (**Exodus 16:4**). God will make a way for you to eat and be healthy if you trust Him. Just ask (**John 14:13**).

However, you will have to work for your daily bread. You can't just sit there and expect **manna** and quail to rain down from heaven.

What use is it, my brothers and sisters, if someone says he has faith, but he has no works? Can that faith save him? If a brother or sister is without clothing and in need of daily food, and one of you says to them, "Go in peace, be warmed and be filled," yet you do not give them what is necessary for their body, what use is that? In the same way, faith also, if it has no works, is dead, being by itself. (James 2:14-17)

Once all of the basic needs, our "daily bread," are met, we are ready to move to the next level of asking. Let's get started on the "I want more" part of the prayer. Time to "upgrade."

I remember when my children were young; we had an old, ragged-looking car. The car ran well and could get me from point A to point B safely. My basic need for transportation was met. But my son would ask me to drop him off a block away from the school. I think he didn't want his newfound friends to see his basic mode of transportation. At that point, all my basic needs were met. My husband and I began praying and looking for the next level, the "upgrade." Of course, asking for the next level meant we needed to work harder and save better. We were able to buy a new mint green minivan. Interestingly, my son was ready for me to pick him up in front of the school. Old car or minivan, either way, our basic needs were met, and I was grateful each step of the way.

There is nothing wrong with wanting more than basic needs. Let's be real—most of us want to live in more than a cardboard house or an adobe-brick house with an outhouse restroom. We want to eat more than just "life-sustaining mush." We would rather have a comfortable means of transportation instead of walking everywhere we go. There is nothing wrong with wanting to be comfortable. We should prosper and be healthy.

Beloved, I pray that in all respects you may prosper and be in good health, just as your soul prospers. (3 John 1:2)

For I know the plans that I have for you, declares the Lord, plans for prosperity and not for disaster, to give you a future and a hope. (Jeremiah 29:11)

God wants us to prosper. But it is not handed to us on a silver platter. We want God to do everything for us, but we don't want to do anything. We want manna and quail-style blessings 24 hours a day, 365 days a year. But the truth is, we must get up and do something to receive the blessings we want.

The soul of the lazy one craves and gets nothing, but the soul of the diligent is made prosperous. (Proverbs 13:4)

Our **"daily bread"** will be provided for us. But we must get up and do something.

God will be with you as you work toward obtaining and maintaining your basic needs. We know God as a provider, Jehovah Jireh. He will guide you and strengthen you on your journey.

For I am the Lord your God who takes hold of your right hand, Who says to you, 'Do not fear, I will help you.' (Isaiah 41:13)

At this point in your prayer journey, you have praised and blessed the name of the Lord. You have sought His will in your life. Now, ask what you will.

If you remain in Me, and My words remain in you, ask whatever you wish, and it will be done for you. (John 15:7)

If you have all of your basic needs met and you are ready for love, belonging, self-esteem, and self-actualization, then go for it! What a blessing it is to be ready to present yourself whole enough to build loving and meaningful relationships with other people.

A person of too many friends comes to ruin, but there is a friend who sticks closer than a brother. (Proverbs 18:24)

When you pray, be focused and know what you are asking for and why. Sometimes we send mixed messages in our prayers. What is your motive? Is it pure?

There are times when we are asking for this, that, or the other, and we are not sure what we want, or we want it for all the wrong reasons.

… You do not have because you do not ask. You ask and do not receive, because you ask with the wrong motives, so that you may spend what you request on your pleasures. (James 4:2-3)

Always take time to think about what you are asking for. Know why you are asking. Be clear about what you need or want and why. Be sure you are not asking "amiss." One preacher I know once jokingly said, "Sometimes we pray 'a-hit and a-mess.'"

As you embark on this week's prayer journey centered around "Daily Bread," remember that attending to your own well-being allows you to better serve others and share the blessings of faith.

Let's get started on a week of "Daily Bread."

Reflection

WEEK 3 / DAY 1

Daily Bread and Beyond
Balancing Necessities and Desires
Give us this day our daily bread. Matthew 6:11

Throughout the day, look at your basic needs. Begin to thank God for meeting each of your basic needs. Call them out one at a time as you come across them. Take time to appreciate how that need is being met. How do you personally define your **"daily bread"** in the context of your current life situation?

Societal expectations or personal ambitions?

Which items from the physiological and safety checklists are you confident you've met, and which are still a concern for you?

Reflection
WEEK 3 / DAY 2
Daily Bread And Beyond
Balancing Necessities And Desires
Give Us This Day Our Daily Bread. Matthew 6:11

What are some examples of things you initially thought you needed but later realized were wants?

How does recognizing the difference between needs and wants influence your daily decisions and priorities?

Reflection

WEEK 3 / DAY 3

Daily Bread and Beyond
Balancing Necessities and Desires
Give us this day our daily bread. Matthew 6:11

Reflect on a time when you felt that your basic needs were miraculously met or provided for. How did that experience impact your trust in God's provision?

How do you balance faith in God's provision with the need for personal effort and responsibility in securing your daily bread?

Reflection

WEEK 3 / DAY 4
Daily Bread and Beyond
Balancing Necessities and Desires
Give us this day our daily bread. Matthew 6:11

How has your social status or background influenced your perspective on what constitutes basic needs and desires?

In what ways do you think your social context affects your goals and aspirations?

Reflection

WEEK 3 / DAY 5
Daily Bread and Beyond
Balancing Necessities and Desires
Give us this day our daily bread. Matthew 6:11

How have technology and advertising shaped your desires and expectations? What strategies do you use to manage these influences?

How can you remain mindful of your true needs in a world that constantly promotes new wants?

Reflection

WEEK 3 / DAY 6

Daily Bread and Beyond
Balancing Necessities and Desires
Give us this day our daily bread. Matthew 6:11

How do you discern whether your prayers focus on fulfilling genuine needs versus desires driven by personal insecurities or societal expectations?

What practices can you incorporate to ensure your prayers are clear and aligned with your needs and values?

Reflection

WEEK 3 / DAY 7

Daily Bread and Beyond
Balancing Necessities and Desires
Give us this day our daily bread. Matthew 6:11

Congratulations! You have focused solely on yourself, your needs, and your wants. That sounds selfish and petty. No, you are not a self-centered narcissist **just** because you spent a week reflecting on your needs. Today is the 7th day of your Daily Bread prayer conversation with God. It is a day of rest. God created the earth in six days. On the seventh day, He rested. Make a point **to** take time today to do something fun or relaxing. Enjoy the day knowing your needs are met.

As you reflect on your prayer journey this week, what resonates with you the most about this experience?

WEEK 4
Transformation Through
Forgiveness

Healing the Heart, Mind, & Soul

And forgive us our debts, as we also have forgiven our debtors. — Matthew 6:12

We often ask God for forgiveness. As humans, we make mistakes. God knows our hearts and is willing to forgive us when we ask. Matthew 6:12 indicates that we must forgive as part of being forgiven.

What does it mean to forgive someone? Does it mean you forgive and forget? Or does it just mean you forgive? What does it look like to forgive? What does it feel like after you forgive? How do you forget? Does the person who committed the offense need to apologize before we grant forgiveness? Or do we simply forgive them? What if the person apologizes and you forgive them? What if they do the same thing again? Does that mean they weren't sorry; therefore, you don't have to forgive them? As you can see, the questions are endless.

Things happen to us throughout life—it's a part of being human. We make mistakes, we wrong people, and we say rude things, sometimes by mistake or on purpose. Later, we realized we were wrong. We want God and people to forgive us.

Then there are those times when people wrong us. They gossip about us, borrow money and never pay it back, lie about us, or commit some other cruel act toward us. We find it hard to forgive them, to let go, and to stop talking about it.

To forgive, as defined by Cambridge Dictionary, means to stop blaming, punishing, or being angry at someone for something that person has done.

We want people to forgive us, yet we often hold grudges for years. This first part of the prayer focuses on letting go—letting go of that hurtful thing someone did to you, letting go of that teacher who was mean to you, letting go of that boss who treated you unjustly. It means no longer being angry, blaming, pointing fingers, or constantly reliving the moment. We have all been hurt by someone or some event. But how do we stop blaming? How do we stop being mad? How do we let go?

When I am hurt by someone or angry with them, I ask myself, "Why am I so angry about that? Why did that hurt my feelings?" If I can identify what triggered the emotion, I can begin to deal with the hurt or anger without confronting the person. By having an honest conversation with God about the problem, I start the process of forgiving and letting go. The best part of these conversations with God is the closer bond I build with Him.

Of course, I will eventually have a conversation with the person about the situation, but the hurt and anger are no longer mixed into the conversation. The more I practice this, the quicker and better I get at it. I answer each of those questions as I talk with God. I allow Him to be a part of the conversation. I allow Him to help heal my hurt. I am comfortable being vulnerable with God. I sometimes cry, laugh, and feel silly during these talks with God. The conversation may take days or weeks.

No one can emotionally hurt you unless you allow it. You can call them out on their behavior without being disrespectful. I have practiced smiling and saying, "How rude." They will try to justify their actions, and I smile some more and say, "But it is insulting." Then I walk off, take a few deep breaths, and let it go. It didn't always come easy. Let's just say it took a few years and a lot of prayers. It does not have to take that long for you. I was strong-willed, sharp-tongued, and laser-focused when I was angry. I am constantly talking with God to hold my peace.

This week's prayer requires that you first learn to forgive. You must stop blaming others and holding grudges. Whatever they did or said was wrong and hurtful. But it is over now, and you cannot allow the incident to hold you hostage. When we hold on to anger or hurt, we become emotionally frozen in time. Negative emotions taint our actions at that point. It is difficult to make good decisions when we are hurt or angry. Finding peace and forgiveness is the key to healing.

Here are some suggestions on ways to let go:

• Create a mantra to say every time you recall the incident. Here are some examples: "The past is the past. I am in the present, looking toward the future." "Oh! I'm not keeping that!" "Not today, Satan." I encourage you to create one that resonates with you.

• Choose a powerful song that will redirect your thoughts. I just started singing "Moving Forward" by Israel Houghton. Even though the lyrics say, "I am not going back," I sing, "I am not looking back." I sing it until it washes every ugly thought from my mind, and I am just thinking about looking and moving forward. Because God makes all things new.

• Do something that makes you laugh. Laughter can indirectly increase endorphins, relieve stress, soothe tension, and improve your mood. My daughter once told me that when she is bored or upset, she starts laughing. At first, it sounds like different silly laughs, but after a while, she laughs at the laughs. I tried it. It works! Now you try it. Stop what you are doing and fake a good, hearty laugh. Look at yourself in the mirror laughing. Set a timer and take a few minutes to laugh. Even Proverbs 17:22 indicates that laughter is good medicine. So, have a good belly laugh at least once a day.

Forgive & Forget

I have a memory like a steel trap. I don't forget. I am 65+ years old and remember events from when I was two years old. Strong emotional events tend to stay in memory longer. So, how do we forget? Cambridge defines forgive and forget as: "To completely stop blaming or being angry with someone for something they did, and to stop thinking about it."

When I read this definition of "forgive and forget," a light switched on in my brain. Just stop talking about it over and over again. Let it go. I have always said I can forgive, meaning I am not angry or upset anymore, but I don't forget. That is true, but I don't have to keep bringing it up or dwelling on it.

We have to forgive, and yes, we have to forget. We have to let go of the hurt and stop bringing it up.

"Bearing with one another, and forgiving each other, whoever has a complaint against anyone; just as the Lord forgave you, so must you do also." — *Colossians 3:13*

We cannot expect to be forgiven if we cannot forgive and forget. This concept is crucial. Jesus restated the importance of forgiving in Matthew 6:14-15. In simple words, "If you want forgiveness, then forgive."

Take a few minutes to let that soak in. Before we begin this week's prayer, we need to face our hurt, anger, and disappointment. Dig deep into your heart and mind.

This is a week of allowing God to help you let go and forgive.

"But Jesus said to him, 'If You can?' All things are possible for the one who believes." — Mark 9:23-24

Let's get started on this week's focused prayer on forgiving. *Let's get ready for a powerful week of talking with God.*

Reflection

WEEK 4 / DAY 1

Transformation Through Forgiveness
Healing the Heart, Mind, & Soul
And forgive us our debts, as we also have forgiven our debtors. - Matthew 6:12

Today's prayer chat with God is about asking Him to help you search your heart. Make a list of past hurts that still linger in your mind and heart. Take another moment to ask yourself why these issues still bother you. Begin to chat with God about them. Tell Him how you feel about the issues, and then begin to let them go, knowing God will take care of them. Resolve in your heart that from this day forward, you will forgive and forget!

Never repay evil for evil to anyone. Respect what is right in the sight of all people. If possible, so far as it depends on you, be at peace with all people. Never take your own revenge, beloved, but leave room for the wrath of God, for it is written: 'Vengeance is Mine, I will repay,' says the Lord. - Romans 12:17-19

What does forgiveness mean to you? How does it align with your understanding of forgiveness described in the chapter?

How do you differentiate between forgiving someone and forgetting what they've done? What are your thoughts on the idea that forgetting is necessary for forgiveness?

Reflection

WEEK 4 / DAY 2

Transformation Through Forgiveness
Healing the Heart, Mind, & Soul
And forgive us our debts, as we also have forgiven our debtors. - Matthew 6:12

Begin this prayer chat by planning your "Letting God Technique" with Him. Chat with God throughout the day, looking for the right song, mantra, scripture, or action that will remind you to stop and let it go. Practice the technique you choose as many times as possible this week. You are not focusing on any of the issues, just the "Letting God Technique."

What personal scriptures, mantras, or affirmations can you use to reinforce the process of letting God?

How can forgiveness free you from emotional burdens and allow you to experience peace?

Reflection

WEEK 4 / DAY 3

Transformation Through Forgiveness
Healing the Heart, Mind, & Soul
And forgive us our debts, as we also have forgiven our
debtors. - Matthew 6:12

Remember that each prayer chat with God should not be a long, dramatic session. Take time today to chat with God about all the fantastic interactions you have had with people or situations. Look for the good in each situation. Allow yourself to smile throughout the day. If memories of an upsetting situation come into your mind, use your "Letting God Technique" to dismiss them.

Do you believe an apology is necessary before forgiveness can be granted?

How does this belief influence your approach to forgiveness?

Reflection

WEEK 4 / DAY 4
Daily Bread and Beyond
Balancing Necessities and Desires
And forgive us our debts, as we also have forgiven our
debtors. - Matthew 6:12

Chat with God about how excited you are about practicing "forgiving and forgetting." Allow Him to begin to heal your past hurts. Trust that He is moving inside your mind and heart. If anything negative enters your mind, push it out using your "Letting God Technique." Continue practicing the technique you have established.

What steps can you take to ensure forgiveness becomes a consistent part of your life?

How do you envision your relationship with God improving as you begin to forgive others and yourself?

Reflection

Daily Bread and Beyond

Balancing Necessities and Desires

And forgive us our debts, as we also have forgiven our debtors. - Matthew 6:12

Life is interesting. Situations tend to repeat. So, let's prepare for the next time a similar situation occurs. Have a prayer chat with God today about ways to avoid or diffuse hostile situations. Don't go over every situation—just the main recurring one. There is always at least one situation in our lives that keeps coming back. We are working on forgetting, but we also need to be proactive. Remember, your first plan may or may not work. Keep discussing it with God until you have a solid plan that works for you.

Is an apology from the person who wronged you necessary for you to grant forgiveness? Why or why not?

How do you respond to repeated offenses from the same person? How does this impact your ability to forgive them?

Reflection

WEEK 4 / DAY 6

Daily Bread and Beyond
Balancing Necessities and Desires
And forgive us our debts, as we also have forgiven our debtors. - Matthew 6:12

We often try to forgive others, but we forget to forgive ourselves. We are not perfect. We make mistakes. Take time today to look in the mirror and forgive the person you see (yourself).

How do you handle situations where someone apologizes but repeats the same offense?

How can you maintain healthy boundaries while practicing forgiveness? How do you balance forgiveness with protecting yourself from recurring offenses?

Reflection

WEEK 4 / DAY 7

Daily Bread and Beyond
Balancing Necessities and Desires
And forgive us our debts, as we also have forgiven our debtors. - Matthew 6:12

You have reached the day of rest. An interesting thing happened when I was writing this section. I meant to write "Letting Go Technique." When I went back to edit, I noticed I had written "Letting God Technique." I had to pause and realize it is difficult to let go of hurt, but I can let God take it. Take time today to reflect and enjoy the presence of God. Jot down the milestones of your journey to forgive.

What is your next step in continuing your journey of forgiveness and forgetting? How can you use the "Letting God Technique?"

In what ways has forgiving or not forgiving others impacted your personal and spiritual development?

WEEK 5

Navigating Temptations

Strengthening Your Spiritual Armor
And do not lead us into temptation, Matthew 6:13a
Ask For Guidance

As Christians, we talk and sing about temptation. I have heard many testimonies in which individuals imply that an external force is causing them to go astray. "This or that tempted me."

The definition of temptation suggests that temptation stems from the individual's desires. Take a moment to let that soak in. "the desires of the individual." You cannot be tempted by something you are not interested in. I do not like 80% dark chocolate. If I am on a diet, I am not tempted to taste or eat it. However, if you place a carrot cake and a cup of tea or coffee in front of me, I would be tempted to eat the whole cake. That desire is within me. It is not the responsibility of the cake baker.

We tend to blame the cake baker instead of owning our shortcomings. My constant prayer is, "Lord, help me avoid my trigger points until I am strong enough to deal with my desires."

Temptation: the wish to do or have something that you know you should not do or have / something that makes you want to do or have something that you know you should not (2)

God does not tempt us. Temptation comes from within us. What may tempt one person may not phase another person. The only thing anyone can do is present situations that pique your interest. How you respond to that is up to you.

No one is to say when he is tempted, "I am being tempted by God"; for God cannot be tempted by evil, and He Himself does not tempt anyone. 14 But each one is tempted when he is carried away and enticed by his own lust. 15 Then when lust has conceived, it gives birth to sin; and sin, when it has run its course, brings forth death. James 1:13-15

When we succumb to temptations, it is easy to blame "the enemy" or others. The truth is that temptation comes from within us. We chose to act on the temptation. The best anyone or any entity can do is to present the item or situation to us. It is up to us to act or refrain from responding.

Jesus was tempted on three levels. The personal reflection on Jesus's temptations adds depth and clarity to our temptations.

Each level of Jesus's temptations coincides with Maslow's Hierarchy of needs.

Level One – Physiological Needs

Physical temptation is a difficult level for many people. You have specific needs and demands that need to be filled. Your body has a powerful pull on how you respond to its needs.

Then Jesus was led up by the Spirit into the wilderness to be tempted by the devil. 2 And after He had fasted for forty days and forty nights, He then became hungry. 3 And the tempter came and said to Him, "If You are the Son of God, command that these stones become bread." 4 But He answered and said, "It is written: 'Man shall not live on bread alone, but on every word that comes out of the mouth of God. Matthew 4:1-4

Jesus was super hungry and very weak due to lack of food. I have read the scriptures regarding Jesus's wilderness experience many times over the last 40 years. I thought, "Of course, he passed the temptation test; he is the Messiah." I now realize he was in human form and had human needs. He was tempted to eat. He was drawn by his own flesh. The key to this is not acting upon temptation. Since we can only be tempted by things we actually want, I believe Jesus wanted to eat but didn't.

I don't know if I could survive 40 days without eating. After one day of not eating, I am "Hangry" and too weak to do anything. At that point, if my grandson left a bag of chips on the counter, I would have difficulty not eating the entire bag.

Fasting is an integral part of developing a mature relationship with God. Our body naturally compels us to respond to our basic needs. When we are thirsty, we naturally get something to drink. When we are hungry, we grab a bite to eat without any thought. To consciously not respond to our body's request takes self-control. This type of self-control will help us when we are in difficult situations. We will have enough control to deal with situations with a disciplined mind.

Being able to address situations with self-control is critical to a successful outcome. Fasting helps control how we respond to situations. It takes practice and time. As a life coach and a youth pastor, I have worked with individuals who want to fast so they can cast out demons. That is a noble desire. Let's start small and work our way up. Sometimes, we struggle with controlling our temper, yet we want to enter spiritual warfare unprepared.

Physical temptations will vary based on the individual's paradigm. We are unique. Whatever your physical temptation may be, know that you can overcome the temptation. You can master self-control!

I can do all things through Him who strengthens me.
Philippians 4:13

No temptation has overtaken you except something common to mankind, and God is faithful, so He will not allow you to be tempted beyond what you are able, but with the temptation will provide the way of escape also, so that you will be able to endure it. 1 Corinthians 10:13

Level Two – Safety, Belonging

Then the devil took Him along into the holy city and had Him stand on the pinnacle of the temple, 6 and he said to Him, "If You are the Son of God, throw Yourself down; for it is written: 'He will give His angels orders concerning You'; and 'On their hands, they will lift You up So that You do not strike Your foot against a stone.'" 7 Jesus said to him, "[a]On the other hand, it is written: 'You shall not put the Lord your God to the test.'" Matthew 4:5-7

This is an interesting temptation. Let's look at this temptation from two sides. In this verse, the term 'tempting' refers to testing God.

Jesus knew he had the power to command angels. Satan was taunting him. "If you are so big and bad, prove it." Or "Let's see if you are all that and the bag of chips!" But Jesus didn't have to prove anything to Satan.

It is comforting to know that God will take care of us. We know that if we call on Him, He will answer. We know He is Jehovah Jireh, our provider; Jehovah Rapha, our healer; and Jehovah Shalom, our provider of peace. We know that if anything happens, He is right there for us. We have a sense of belonging, love, and friendship. We also know He has given us the power to cast out demons and to tread on serpents. Matthew 10:l, Mark 3:14-15,

Sometimes, we want God to fix a situation when he has given us the power to fix it ourselves. There are times when we truly need Him to step in and help, and there are times when we need to fix our mess.

When we ask God not to lead us into temptation, let us not walk toward temptation. We have the power to walk away.

Level Three – Self-Actualization, Greed & Power

Again, the devil took Him along to a very high mountain and showed Him all the kingdoms of the

world and their glory; 9 and he said to Him, "All these things I will give You if You fall down and worship me." 10 Then Jesus said to him, "Go away, Satan! For it is written: 'You shall worship the Lord your God, and serve Him only.'" 11 Then the devil left Him; and behold, angels came and began to serve Him. Matthew 4:8-11

Notice how power keeps popping up. This time, it is coupled with greed. Once our basic needs are met, we want more. We all want to look good and have nice things. In today's world, many of us want to be well-known on social media. Likes, friends, followers, etc. What are we willing to do to get the recognition?

Jesus had the power to command all the elements on earth and the angels. He can command and control even Satan. Yet he used self-restraint. He knew his purpose and remained focused on the end goal. This was not the time or place to show his power.

This is a challenging temptation for many of us. We live in a society of entitlement. We are frustrated when we are passed over for a promotion. We want everyone to know how intelligent, pretty, and fantastic we are. We meet people, and the second or third sentence they say is their resume.

There is nothing wrong with wanting people to respect you. You should be valued for who you are and what you do. Finding the balance is the key. Jesus knew it was not time for a display of power.

Preparing for Temptation

Jesus prepared himself for the temptation in several ways. By studying the Word of God and by fasting. Paul encouraged Timothy to study the Word of God. 2 Timothy 2:15

We overcome temptation by learning to control our flesh. Fasting denies our body of basic needs. As our body screams to be fed, we hold steadfast in not eating. This simple act of denial is powerful.

When was the last time you fasted? I am not talking about the two-hour fast or the type of fast when you give up one item. I am talking about denying your body food until it screams at you. It is the type of fast where your stomach aches for food, and you don't want to do anything but eat.

This week, we will pray for temptation preparation. This may be the hardest prayer week. When you target a weak spot and begin to pray, it always feels like it gets worse before it gets better. Don't give up.

The second way Jesus prepared for temptation was by studying the Word of God. Jesus quoted scriptures when he was tempted. To use the Word of God to combat temptation, you will need to know and understand the Word of God.

There is a difference between reading the Word and studying the Word. When you study, you develop a deeper understanding. You know what the scripture means and how to use it in battle. I know samurai swords cut. However, I need to learn how to use one properly. I can hack my way through something using the samurai sword without instructions. I may successfully cut down a bush. If I learned the proper use and techniques of the sword, I may realize I should use a machete or a chainsaw to do the job.

Knowing what scripture to use and when makes all the difference in your success level during temptation.

As we begin this prayer, remember the following scripture.

No temptation has overtaken you except something common to mankind, and God is faithful, so He will not allow you to be tempted beyond what you are able, but with the temptation will provide the way of escape also, so that you will be able to endure it. 1 Corinthians 10:13

You can overcome all temptations by reading God's word, fasting, praying, and trusting God.

Reflection

WEEK 5 - DAY 1

Navigating Temptations

Strengthening Your Spiritual Armor

And do not lead us into temptation, Matthew 6:13a

Week 5 Day 1

Chat with God today about areas of your life where you are tempted. Take time to think about why you are tempted. You are human, so don't be too hard on yourself. Chat with God about one area to focus on this week.

How do you relate to the idea that temptation stems from your desires?

Can you identify a recent situation where you felt tempted? What were the underlying desires or motivations at play?

Reflection

WEEK 5 DAY 2

Navigating Temptations

Strengthening Your Spiritual Armor

And do not lead us into temptation, Matthew 6:13a

Begin a limited fast by giving up a specific favorite food for the day. This prayer journey is about your self-development. Choose an area of your spiritual life you want to develop. Throughout the day, chat with God about why you are fasting. Remember that a conversation goes two ways. God reviles Himself in many ways.

What did you discover during the fast and chats today?

Consider the role of fasting in developing self-control. How has fasting or other self-discipline impacted your ability to resist temptation?

Reflection

WEEK 5 DAY 3

Navigating Temptations

Strengthening Your Spiritual Armor

And do not lead us into temptation, Matthew 6:13a

Continue to focus on building your resistance to acting on temptations. You may choose to continue a modified fast, or you may choose a longer fast. Either way, God will see that you are taking steps to strengthen your physical and spiritual discipline. Remember to take time throughout the day to pause and chat with God on a walk or sit and relax during the chat.

What steps or actions can you take to minimize your expenses to some of the temptations?

How does being part of a community like a church affect your ability to handle temptations?

Reflection

WEEK 5 DAY 4

Navigating Temptations

Strengthening Your Spiritual Armor

And do not lead us into temptation, Matthew 6:13a

You have denied your physical needs for two days. Today take time to reflect on the experience. You focused on an area of temptation during the fast. Begin to chat with God about how to use His word to strengthen you during temptation. Jot the scriptures down and begin saying them throughout the rest of the week. The more you say them the deeper into you they become. They will become a part of you. Psalms 119:11.

What scriptures resonate with you when dealing with specific temptations? Ask God to help you select the scriptures that best meet your needs.

In your own words what do those scriptures mean to you?

Reflection

WEEK 5 DAY 5

Navigating Temptations

Strengthening Your Spiritual Armor

And do not lead us into temptation, Matthew 6:13a

Read the scriptures you selected on day 4 and meditate on them. Chat with God about what each of the scriptures means and how they relate to you.

Can you recall a time when you successfully aligned your actions with your spiritual goals despite facing strong temptations?

Take time to rejoice in overcoming the temptation. What key practices did you have in place at that time? How can you continue to strengthen those practices?

Reflection

WEEK 5 DAY 6

Navigating Temptations

Strengthening Your Spiritual Armor

And do not lead us into temptation, Matthew 6:13a

Read Psalm 1: 1-6. Throughout the day, have an honest chat with God about your walk with Him. You want to be the tree planted by the rivers of water. What is holding you back? Allow God the show you what you need to do to strengthen your spirit.

How does Jesus's response to temptation inspire you in dealing with your challenges? What is one thing you learned from His approach?

In what ways do you relate to the different levels of temptation Jesus faced?

Reflection

WEEK 5 DAY 7

Navigating Temptations

Strengthening Your Spiritual Armor

And do not lead us into temptation, Matthew 6:13a

You have reached the day of rest! This was a powerful week. Facing temptations, fasting, reading the Bible, and facing your flaws. Let's just breathe today. Allow God to comfort you and encourage you. Let go and let God pamper you for a day.

Take time today to reflect and enjoy the presence of God. Journal your highs and lows of the week. Know that God WILL be there for you in every situation. Isaiah 41:10

What are some long-term strategies you can
implement to build resilience against temptation?

How can fasting, praying, and studying the Word
become regular practices in your life?

A God Chat

WEEK 6

Navigating Life's Storms with Faith and Resilience

Trusting God Amidst Adversity

... but deliver us from evil: Matthew 6:13b

Seeking Deliverance

There are times in our lives when the enemy is attacking us or our family solely because we are trying to follow the will of God. These are the times when we call for divine intervention. David became a target of the king's wrath because the king saw him as a threat. David was walking in the will and anointing of God, yet he had to run and hide. He learned to trust God. However, that did not mean the situation turned around the next day.

It is not easy when people come against you. Facing opposition is always challenging. It is difficult to be still and allow God to fight the battle.

Lord, how my enemies have increased!
Many are rising up against me. 2 Many
are saying of my soul, "There is no
salvation for him in God." Selah 3 But
You, Lord, are a shield around me, My
glory, and the One who lifts my head.
Psalms 3:1-3

"Why do bad things happen to good people?" Life happens to all of us. People become frustrated when bad things happen. Yes, sometimes we cause it ourselves. But there are times when we did nothing wrong.

Cain and Abel were brothers. **Genesis 3** I like to think they grew up laughing and playing together. Perhaps their parents, Adam and Eve, taught them to worship God. Each son worshipped God in their way. Abel was a herdsman. Abel's sacrifice was with blood. Cain was a farmer. Cain's sacrifice was fruit.

> ***And almost all things are cleansed with***
> ***blood, according to the Law, and***
> ***without the shedding of blood, there is***
> ***no forgiveness. Hebrews 9:22***

I sometimes jokingly say, "It looks like God didn't want kale & beet juice or a strawberry banana smoothie." Beet juice is red but is not a blood sacrifice and cannot wash away sin.

All joking aside, Cain was jealous and ultimately killed Abel. What did Abel do to desire death by his brother's hand? Nothing! Sometimes, bad things happen to good people.

Joseph was a dreamer, and his father loved him dearly. Joseph had 11 brothers. Joseph told his brothers about a dream he had, and his brothers were jealous, so they sold him. What did Joseph do wrong? Nothing!

Joseph went through several bad situations before God opened doors for him. **Genesis 37-50.**

God sees the injustices done to you. He knows when it is not your fault. He will strengthen you and be there with you.

There was a time when I was surrounded by people who hated me. They did everything to destroy my character. They accused me of doing things I never would have thought of doing. This went on for several years.

Some may say I brought it on myself. Others may say I was a threat to their success or other reasons. It does not matter. I tried to fix it myself, and that turned out terrible. It worked out when I let go and allowed God to fight the battle. I learned not to jump into a fight that does not belong to me. The battle is the Lords. Oh, I cried many nights while I was "being still." It hurt to watch and know how hated I was. But, God will deliver His children from evil in due time.

People often project their characteristics onto others. When you know you have not done wrong, allow God to defend you. If we allow God, he will bring all things to light.

There are hurricanes, earthquakes, tornados, tsunamis, hailstorms, rain, shootings, Covid, cancer, and so many tragedies. Sometimes, good people die in tragedies. Sometimes, bad people survive tragedies. That is life. Just because we are children of the Most High does not mean we get unlimited "get out of jail free" cards. We get caught in the storms of life just like everyone else.

> *...He causes His sun to rise on the evil and the good and sends rain on the righteous and the unrighteous.*
> *Matthew 5:45*

It is not the tragedies of life that define us but how we respond. We have peace amid tears and turmoil. We know God is with us in the storm.

"What if trials of this life, the rain, the storms the hardest nights are His mercies in disguise? (Blessings – Laura Story.)"

When we cry out to God he hears our cries. He will deliver us out of the storms of life. It is not always the way we want but He will deliver us.

I would love to have powerful, comforting words for you during the storms of life. But the truth is, the words, comfort, and peace come from knowing that God is your fortress, your strong tower in the storm. It is nice to have people be there to hold your hand, pray, and sit with you. But when they go home, you are not alone. God is there.

Chatting with God daily builds a strong relationship with Him. This relationship is what will carry you through the bad storms of life.

As young adults, my children went through rough patches of life like most children. I lost weight while praying and fasting for them. No matter how sad I felt or all the nights of tears, I never for one minute felt God would not carry them through this phase of their lives. Feeling sad or stressed does not mean you do not trust God. God did step in, and I am overjoyed to see the amazing adults they are today. To God be all the glory and honor! Never stop praying for your family. Never give up.

Bad things happen to all of us, no matter how we try to avoid them. It rains on all of us. God's children have an umbrella. Oh, we get wet, but we don't get drenched. Do not be quick to look for blame or wrongdoing. Job's friends were sure he did something wrong to desire the troubles he experienced. Job had his moments of frustration, but in the end, God blessed him.

Stand tall and keep putting one foot in front of the other during hard times. Trust God to be your fortress. Know that he will deliver you.

Reflection

WEEK 6 / Day 1

Navigating Life's Storms with Faith and Resilience

Trusting God Amidst Adversity

… but deliver us from evil: Matthew 6:13b

Reflect on the hard times of your life. Think about how God was there during your struggles. During your God Chat today, talk about the situation.

Looking back at past difficulties, how have they contributed to your personal and spiritual growth?

What positive changes have you noticed in yourself due to these experiences?

Reflection

WEEK 6 / Day 2

Navigating Life's Storms with Faith and Resilience

Trusting God Amidst Adversity

... but deliver us from evil: Matthew 6:13b

What storm are you going through at this time in your life? What do you feel he is saying to you as you chat with God about this current storm? Remember, the chat is a two-way conversation. You talk – God listens; God talks – you listen.

What does "being still and allowing God to fight the battle" look like practically in your life?

How do self-reflection and self-examination affect your response to trials? How do you discern whether challenges are a result of personal actions or external factors?

Reflection

WEEK 6 / Day 3

Navigating Life's Storms with Faith and Resilience

Trusting God Amidst Adversity

... but deliver us from evil: Matthew 6:13b

Read Romans 8:28

During your God Chat, share your thoughts about this scripture with God. Is there a situation where you are struggling to see the good?

How can you approach it with a more trusting heart?

How do you reconcile the existence of suffering and difficulties with the belief that God is just and loving?

How does this understanding influence your view of personal trials?

Reflection

WEEK 6 / Day 4

Navigating Life's Storms with Faith and Resilience

Trusting God Amidst Adversity

… but deliver us from evil: Matthew 6:13b

Read Romans 5:3-5

During today's God Chat, share your thoughts about these scriptures with God.

How do you typically respond when faced with unexpected or unfair hardships? Do you find it difficult to rejoice in times of suffering? Why or why not?

What steps do you take to trust God during difficult times, especially when it seems like the situation is not improving quickly?

Reflection

WEEK 6 / Day 5

Navigating Life's Storms with Faith and Resilience

Trusting God Amidst Adversity

... but deliver us from evil: Matthew 6:13b

Read Isaiah 54:17

During today's God Chat share your thoughts about these scriptures with God. What are the "weapons" that might be formed against you in your life? (Challenges, opposition, doubt, injustice, etc)

How can this verse help you navigate those difficulties?

Reflecting on the stories of David, Joseph, and others, how have their experiences influenced your perspective on personal growth through adversity?

Reflection

WEEK 6 / Day 6

Navigating Life's Storms with Faith and Resilience
Trusting God Amidst Adversity
… but deliver us from evil: Matthew 6:13b

Read James 1:3-4

Throughout this week, you had powerful chats with God about your problems, trials, and other injustices in your life.

How has your relationship with God been impacted by your trials?

In what ways has your faith been strengthened or challenged during these times?

Reflection

WEEK 6 / Day 7

Navigating Life's Storms with Faith and Resilience

Trusting God Amidst Adversity

… but deliver us from evil: Matthew 6:13b

You have reached the day of rest! Just breathe today. Allow God to comfort you and encourage you. On the seventh day, God rested. What are the highlights of Genesis 2:2 As you reflect on this week?

What did you learn about how you respond to bad things happening?

As you look to the future, how does your faith in God's deliverance and protection influence your outlook on life's uncertainties?

What practical steps can you take to build resilience and faith in preparation for future challenges? How can you apply the lessons you have learned from past trials to current or future situations?

WEEK 7

Rest, Reflect, Medicate & Listen
Trusting God Amidst Adversity
… but deliver us from evil: Matthew 6:13b
Rest, Reflection, Meditation

Throughout this prayer journey, you may have noticed that I believe in a day of rest. By resting your body and mind, you enter into a receptive state. You are calm and centered. You can hear the will of God in your life.

You have taken a six-week journey to strengthen your relationship with God. You have focused on chatting with Him and listening to him. Some days was easy to hear God, and other days you may have struggled to listen to His voice.

There are many forms of prayer. The most important form is when an individual can have a two-way conversation with God. Those are my prayers that get the most results. My daily God Chats are filled with laughter, tears, anger, joy, sorrow, and sometimes just a non-emotional chat about life. There are times I am just annoyed about something. I will fuss and complain about the entire situation with God. He listens, and somehow, by the end of my rant, He has calmed my soul. By the end of every chat, I am in total adoration of His power and love for me.

This is a week of rest, reflection, meditation, and listening. Be still and know that He is God. Listen for the still voice. Notice the message in the storm.

This week's challenge is to say the entire Lord's prayer each day. Each day rise out of bed wash your face, find a quiet place, and take a moment to start the day praying the model prayer, "The Lord's Prayer."

As you pray, think about what each verse means in your life. There are other Biblical translations of the Lord's Prayer. You may choose any translation that resonates with you. It does not have to be the King

James version or the New American Standard Bible version.

Matthew 6:9-13

Our Father, who is in heaven, Hallowed be Your name. Your kingdom come. Your will be done, On earth as it is in heaven. Give us this day our daily bread. And forgive us our debts, as we also have forgiven our debtors. And do not lead us into temptation, but deliver us from evil. For Yours is the kingdom and the power and the glory forever. Amen

King James Version

Our Father which art in heaven, Hallowed be thy name. Thy kingdom come, Thy will be done in earth, as it is in heaven. Give us this day our daily bread. And forgive us our debts, as we forgive our debtors. And lead us not into temptation, but deliver us from evil: For thine is the kingdom, and the power, and the glory, forever. Amen.

Reflection

Week 7 / Day 1

Rest / Reflect / Meditate / Listen

After you pray the Lord's prayer. What does this section of the prayer mean to you? Write the following section of the Lord's Prayer in your own words.

Our Father who is in heaven, Hallowed be your name. Matthew 6:9

Reflection

Week 7 / Day 2

Rest / Reflect / Meditate / Listen

After you pray the Lord's prayer. What does this section of the prayer mean to you? Write the following section of the Lord's Prayer in your own words.

Your Kingdom come. Your will be done, On earth as it is in heaven. Matthew 6:10

Reflection

Week 7 / Day 3

Rest / Reflect / Meditate / Listen

After you pray the Lord's prayer. What does this section of the prayer mean to you? Write the following section of the Lord's Prayer in your own words.

Give us this day our daily bread. Matthew 6:11

Reflection

Week 7 / Day 4

Rest / Reflect / Meditate / Listen

After you pray the Lord's prayer. What does this section of the prayer mean to you? Write the following section of the Lord's Prayer in your own words.

And forgive us our debts, as we also have forgiven our debtors. Matthew 6:12

Reflection

Week 7 / Day 5

Rest / Reflect / Meditate / Listen

After you pray the Lord's prayer. What does this section of the prayer mean to you? Write the following section of the Lord's Prayer in your own words.

And do not lead us into temptation, Matthew 6:13a

Reflection

Week 7 / Day 6

Rest / Reflect / Meditate / Listen

After you pray the Lord's prayer. What does this section of the prayer mean to you? Write the following section of the Lord's Prayer in your own words.

...deliver us from evil Matthew 6:13b

Reflection

Week 7 / Day 7

Rest / Reflect / Meditate / Listen

After you pray the Lord's prayer. What does this section of the prayer mean to you? Write the following section of the Lord's Prayer in your own words.

For Yours is the kingdom and the power and the glory forever. Amen Matthew 6:13c

CONCLUSION

Prayer is more than just a ritual or a list of requests—it is an ongoing, heartfelt conversation with God. Throughout this book, we have explored different styles of prayer, using the Lord's Prayer as our guide. We have seen that prayer is not about the perfect words or a specific formula but about sincere communication with our Creator. Whether through praise, confession, thanksgiving, or supplication, each prayer deepens our relationship with Him.

As you have walked through this journey, I hope you have discovered new ways to connect with God—ways that feel personal and meaningful to you. Perhaps you have found joy in journaling your prayers, peace in silent reflection, or strength in lifting up your concerns with confidence. Prayer is not a one-size-fits-all practice; it is a dynamic and evolving relationship.

Remember, prayer is not about perfection—it's about presence. God does not require eloquence or lengthy speeches; He desires our hearts. Keep talking to Him, keep listening, and most importantly, keep growing in faith. There will be days when prayer feels effortless and days when it feels like a struggle, but through it all, God is always near, always listening, and always faithful.

As you continue your prayer journey, I encourage you to remain committed to making prayer a daily habit. Set aside time, find your quiet place, and most of all, be open to hearing God's voice. Let prayer be the foundation of your faith, the source of your strength, and the path to a deeper, richer relationship with Christ.

May you be blessed in your journey, and may your conversations with God continue to transform your heart and life.

Amen.

I want to encourage you to find a place to fellowship.

Behold, how good and how pleasant it is for brothers to live together in unity! Psalms 133:1.

Let's consider how to encourage one another in love and good deeds, 25 not abandoning our own meeting together, as is the habit of some people, but encouraging one another; and all the more as you see the day drawing near. Hebrews 10:24-25
As iron sharpens iron, so one person sharpens another. Proverbs 27:17

Reference

1. Maslow's Hierarchy of Needs by Saul Meleod, PhD, Updated on January 24, 2024, Reviewed by Olivia Guy Evans
https://www.simplypsychology.org/maslow.html

2. Cambridge University Press & Assessment 2024,
https://dictionary.cambridge.org/us/dictionary/english/hallowed

3. https://dictionary.cambridge.org/us/dictionary/english/forgive

4. Merriam-Webster, Incorporated,
https://www.merriam-webster.com/dictionary/amiss

Mayo Clinic, Stress Management,
https://www.mayoclinic.org/healthy-lifestyle/stress-management/in-depth/stress-relief

www.ingramcontent.com/pod-product-compliance
Lightning Source LLC
LaVergne TN
LVHW051409080426
835508LV00022B/3004

* 9 7 9 8 9 9 2 4 4 4 5 0 6 *